SELECT COMMITTEE TO
INVESTIGATE THE

JANUARY 6TH

ATTACK ON THE
UNITED STATES CAPITOL

First Select Committee Hearing
June 9, 2022

COMPLETE TRANSCRIPT

-As Delivered-

Bennie Thompson: "The Select Committee to investigate the January 6th attack on a United States Capitol will be in order. Without objection, the chair is authorized to declare the committee in recess at any point. Pursuant to House Deposition Authority Regulation 10, the chair announces the committee's approval to release the deposition material presented during tonight's hearing. Thanks to everyone watching tonight for sharing part of your evening to learn the facts and causes of the events leading up to and including the violent attack on January 6th, 2021, our democracy, electoral system, and country. I'm Bennie Thompson, chairman of the January 6th, 2021 committee. I was born, raised, and still live in Bolton, Mississippi, a town with a population of 521, which is midway between Jackson and Vicksburg, Mississippi and the Mississippi River. I'm from a part of the country where people justify the actions of slavery, the Klu Klux Klan, and lynching. I'm reminded of that dark history as I hear voices today try and justify the actions of the insurrectionists on January 6th, 2021.

"Over the next few weeks, hopefully you will get to know the other members, my colleagues up here, and me. We represent a diversity of communities from all over the United States, rural areas and cities, East Coast, West Coast and the heartland. All of us have one thing in common. We swore the same oath, that same old that all members of Congress take up on taking office and, afterwards, every two years if they are reelected. We swore an oath to defend the Constitution against all enemies, foreign and domestic. The words of the current oath taken by all of us, that nearly every United States government employee takes, have their roots in the Civil War.

"Throughout our history, the United States has fought against foreign enemies to preserve our democracy, electoral system, and country. When the United States Capitol was stormed and burned in 1814, foreign enemies were responsible. Afterward, in 1862, when American citizens had taken up arms against this country, Congress adopted a new oath to help make sure no person who had supported the rebellion could hold a position of public trust. Therefore, Congresspersons and United States federal government employees were required for the first time to swear an oath to defend the Constitution against all enemies, foreign and domestic. That oath was put to test on January 6th, 2021. The police officers who held the line that day honored their oath. Many came out of that day bloodied and broken. They still bear those wounds, visible and invisible. They did their duty. They repelled the mob and ended the occupation of the Capitol. They defended the Constitution against domestic enemies so that Congress could return, uphold our own oath, and count your votes to ensure the transfer of power, just as we've done for hundreds of years.

"But unlike in 1814, it was domestic enemies of the Constitution who stormed the Capitol and occupied the Capitol, who sought to thwart the will of the people, to stop the transfer of power. And so, they did so at the encouragement of the president of the United States, the president of the United States trying to stop the transfer of power, a precedent that had stood for 220 years, even as our democracy had faced its most difficult test.

"Thinking back again to the Civil War, in the summer of 1864 the president of the United States believed he — he would be doomed to bid — his bid for reelection. He believed his opponent, General George McClellan, would wave the white flag when it came to preserving the union. "But even with that grim fate hanging in the balance, President Lincoln was ready to accept the will of the voters, come what may. He made a quiet pledge. He wrote down the words, 'This morning, as for some days past, it seems exceedingly probable that this administration will not be reelected. Then it will be my duty to so cooperate with the president elect. It will be my duty.'

"Lincoln sealed that memo and asked his cabinet secretaries to sign it sight unseen. He asked them to make the same commitment he did, to accept defeat if indeed defeat was the will of the people, to uphold the rule of law, to do what every president who came before him did, and what every president who followed him would do, until Donald Trump. Donald Trump lost the presidential election in 2020. The American people voted him out of office. It was not because of a rigged system. It was not because of voter fraud. Don't believe me? Hear what his former attorney general had to say about it. I warn those who — watching that this content contains strong language."

[multimedia]

William Barr: "No, just what I — I've been — I've had — I had three discussions with the president that I can recall. One was on November 23rd, one was on December 1st, and one was on December 14th. And I've been through sort of the give and take of those discussions. And in that context, I made it clear I did not agree with the idea of saying the election was stolen and putting out this stuff, which I told the president was bullshit. And, you know, I didn't want to be a part of it, and that's one of the reasons that went into me deciding to leave when I did. I observed, I think it was on December 1st, that, you know, how can we — you can't live in a world where — where the incumbent administration stays in power based on its view, unsupported by specific evidence, that the election — that there was fraud in the election."

Bennie Thompson: "Bill Barr, on Election Day 2020, he was the attorney general of the United States, the top law enforcement official in the country, telling the president exactly what he thought about claims of a stolen election. Donald Trump had his days in court to challenge the results. He was within his rights to seek those judgment in the United States. Law abiding citizens have those tools for pursuing justice. He lost in the courts, just as he did at the ballot box. And in this country, that's the end of the line. But for Donald Trump, that was only the beginning of what became a sprawling multistep conspiracy aimed at overturning the presidential election, aimed at throwing out the votes of millions of Americans, your votes, your voice in our democracy, and replacing the will of the American people with his will to remain in power after his term ended. Donald Trump was at the center of this conspiracy, and ultimately Donald Trump, the president of the United States, spurred a mob of domestic enemies of the Constitution to march down the Capitol and subvert American democracy.

"Any legal jargon you hear about seditious conspiracy, obstruction of an official proceeding, conspiracy to defraud the United States boils down to this. January 6th was the culmination of an attempted coup, a brazen attempt, as one rioter to put it shortly after January 6th, to overthrow the government. The violence was no accident. It represents seeing Trump's last stand, most desperate chance to halt the transfer of power.

"Now, you may hear those words and think this is just another political attack on Donald Trump by people who don't like him. That's not the case. My colleagues and I all wanted an outside independent commission to investigate January 6th, similar to what we had after 9/11. But after first agreeing to the idea, Donald Trump's allies in Congress put a stop to it. Apparently, they don't want January 6th investigated at all. And in the last 17 months, many of those same people have tried to whitewash what happened on January 6th, to rewrite history, call it a tourist visit, label it legitimate political discourse.

"Donald Trump and his followers have adopted the words of the songwriter, do you believe me or your lying eyes? We can't sweep what happened under the rug. The American people deserve answers, so I come before you this evening not as a Democrat, but as an American who swore an oath to defend the Constitution.

"The Constitution doesn't protect just Democrats or just Republicans. It protects all of us, we, the people. And this scheme was an attempt to undermine the will of the people.

"So, tonight and over the next few weeks, we're going to remind you of the reality of what happened that day, but our work must do much more than just look backwards. The cause of our democracy remains in danger. The conspiracy to thwart the will of the people is not over. There are those in this audience who thirst for power, but have no love or respect for what makes America great, devotion to the Constitution, allegiance to the rule of law, our shared journey to build a more perfect union. January 6th and the lies that led to insurrection have put two and a half centuries of constitutional democracy at risk.

"The world is watching what we do here. America has long been expected to be a shining city on the hill, a beacon of hope and freedom, a model for others when we are at our best. How can we play that role when our house is in such disorder? We must confront the truth with candor, resolve, and determination.

"We need to show that we are worthy of the gifts that are the birthright of every American. That begins here and it begins now, with a true accounting of what happened and what led to the attack on our Constitution and our democracy. In this moment, when the dangers of our Constitution and our democracy loom large, nothing could be more important. Working alongside the public servants on this dais has been one of the greatest honors of my time in Congress. It's been a particular privilege to count as a partner in this effort and to count as a friend the gentlewoman from Wyoming, Ms. Cheney. She's a patriot, a public servant of profound courage, of devotion to her oath and the Constitution. It's my pleasure to recognize Ms. Cheney for her opening statement."

Liz Cheney: "Thank you very much, Mr. Chairman. And let me echo those words about the importance of — of bipartisanship and what a tremendous honor it is to work on this committee. Mr. Chairman, at 6:01 p.m. on January 6th, after he spent hours watching a violent mob besiege, attack, and invade our Capitol, Donald Trump tweeted, but he did not condemn the attack. Instead, he justified it. These are the things and events that happen, he said, when a sacred landslide election victory is so unceremoniously and viciously stripped away from great patriots who have been badly and unfairly treated for so long.

"As you will see in the hearings to come, President Trump believed his supporters at the Capitol, and I quote, 'were doing what they should be doing.' This is what he told his staff as they pleaded with him to call off the mob, to instruct his supporters to leave. Over a series of hearings in the coming weeks, you will hear testimony, live and on video, from more than half a dozen former White House staff in the Trump administration, all of whom were in the West Wing of the White House on January 6th. You will hear testimony that, 'The president did not really want to put anything out calling off the riot or asking his supporters to leave.' You will hear that President Trump was yelling and 'really angry' at advisers who told him he needed to be doing something more. And aware of the rioters' chants to hang Mike Pence, the president responded with this sentiment, 'Maybe our supporters have the right idea.' Mike Pence 'deserves it.'"

Liz Cheney: "You will hear evidence that President Trump refused for hours to do what his staff and his family and many of his other advisers begged him to do, immediately instruct his supporters to stand down and evacuate the Capitol. Tonight, you will see never before seen footage of the brutal attack on our Capitol. An attack that unfolded while a few blocks away President Trump sat watching television in the dining room next to the Oval Office.

"You will hear audio from the brave police officers battling for their lives and ours, fighting to defend our democracy against a violent mob Donald Trump refused to call off. Tonight and in the weeks to come, you will see evidence of what motivated this violence including directly from those who participated in this attack. You will see video of them explaining what caused them to do it. You will see their posts on social media. We will show you what they have said in federal court. On this point, there is no room for debate. Those who invaded our capital and battled law enforcement for hours were motivated by what President Trump had told them, that the election was stolen and that he was the rightful President. President Trump summoned the mob, assembled the mob, and lit the flame of this attack. You will also hear about plots to commit seditious conspiracy on January 6th, a crime defined in our laws as conspiring to overthrow, put down, or destroy by force the government of the United States or to oppose by force the authority thereof.

"Multiple members of two groups, the Oath Keepers and the Proud Boys have been charged with this crime for their involvement in the events leading up to and on January 6th. Some have pled guilty. The attack on our Capitol was not a spontaneous riot. Intelligence available before January 6th identified plans to quote, 'invade the Capitol, occupy the Capitol, and take other steps to halt Congress's count of electoral votes that day'. In our hearings to come, we will identify elements of those plans and we will show specifically how a group of Proud Boys led a mob into the Capitol building on January 6th. Tonight, I am going to describe for you some of what our committee has learned and highlight initial findings you will see this month in our hearings. As you hear this, all Americans should keep in fact — in mind this fact. On the morning of January 6th, President Donald Trump's intention was to remain President of the United States despite the lawful outcome of the 2020 election and in violation of his constitutional obligation to relinquish power. Over multiple months, Donald Trump oversaw and coordinated a sophisticated seven part plan to overturn the Presidential election and prevent the transfer of Presidential power.

"In our hearings, you will see evidence of each element of this plan. In our second hearing, you will see that Donald Trump and his advisers knew that he had in fact lost the election. But despite this, President Trump engaged in a massive effort to spread false and fraudulent information to convince huge portions of the US population that fraud had stolen the election from him. This was not true. Jason Miller was a senior Trump campaign spokesman. In this clip, Miller describes a call between the Trump campaign's internal data expert and President Trump a few days after the 2020 election."

[multimedia]
Jason Miller: "I was in the Oval Office and at some point in the conversation Matt Oczkowski, who was the lead data person was brought on and I remember he delivered to the President pretty blunt terms that he was going to lose."

Unknown: "And that was based, Mr. Miller, on Matt and the data team's assessment of the

sort of county by county, state by state results as reported?"

Jason Miller: "Correct."

Liz Cheney: "Alex Cannon was one of President Trump's campaign lawyers. He previously worked for the Trump Organization. One of his responsibilities was to assess allegations of election fraud in November 2020. Here is one sample of his testimony discussing what he told White House Chief of Staff, Mark Meadows."

[multimedia]
Alex Cannon: "I remember a call with Mr. Meadows where Mr. Meadows was asking me what I was finding. And if I was finding anything. And I remember sharing with him that we weren't finding anything that would be sufficient to change the results in any of the key states."

Unknown: "When was that conversation?"

Alex Cannon: "Probably in November, mid to late November. I think it was before my child was born."

Unknown: "And what was Mr. Meadows reaction to that information?"

Alex Cannon: "I believe the words he used were, so there's no there there."

Liz Cheney: "There's no there there. The Trump campaign's general counsel, Matt Morgan, gave similar testimony. He explained that all of the fraud allegations and the campaign's other election arguments taken together and viewed in the best possible light for President Trump could still not change the outcome of the election.

President Trump's Attorney General, Bill Barr, also told Donald Trump his election claims were wrong."

> [multimedia]
> **William Barr: "Repeatedly told the President in no uncertain terms that I did not see evidence of fraud. And — you know, that would have affected the outcome of the election. And frankly a year and a half later, I haven't seen anything to change my mind on that."**

Liz Cheney: "Attorney General Barr also told President Trump that his allegations about Dominion voting machines were groundless."

> [multimedia]
> **William Barr: "I saw absolutely zero basis for the allegations, but they were made in such a sensational way that they obviously were influencing a lot of people, members of the public that there was this systemic corruption in the system and that their votes didn't count and that these machines controlled by somebody else were actually determining it, which was complete nonsense. And it was being laid out there. And I told them that it was — that it was crazy stuff and they were wasting their time on that. And it was doing a great, grave disservice to the country."**

Liz Cheney: "But President Trump persisted, repeating the false Dominion allegations in public at least a dozen more times even after his Attorney General told him, they were quote, 'complete nonsense'. And after Barr's resignation on December 23rd, the acting Attorney General who replaced him, Jeff Rosen, and the acting deputy, Richard Donoghue, told President Trump over and over again that the evidence did not support allegations he was making in public. Many of President Trump's White House staff also recognized that the evidence did not support the claims President Trump was making. This is the President's daughter commenting on Bill Barr's statement that the department found no fraud sufficient to overturn the election."

> **[multimedia]**
> **Unknown: "How did that affect your perspective about the election when Attorney General Barr made that statement?"**
>
> **Ivanka Trump: "It affected my perspective. I respect Attorney General Barr. So I accepted what he was saying."**

Liz Cheney: "As you will hear on Monday, the President had every right to litigate his campaign claims, but he ultimately lost more than 60 cases in state and federal courts. The President's claims in the election cases were so frivolous and unsupported that the President's lead lawyer, Rudy Giuliani, not only lost the lawsuits, his license to practice law was suspended. Here is what the court said of Mr. Giuliani. Giuliani communicated demonstrably false and misleading statements to courts, lawmakers, and the public at large in his capacity as lawyer for former President Donald J Trump and the Trump campaign in connection with Trump's failed effort at reelection in 2020.

"As you will see in great detail in our hearings, President Trump ignored the rulings of our nation's courts. He ignored his own campaign leadership, his White House staff, many Republican state officials. He ignored the Department of Justice and the Department of Homeland Security. President Trump invested millions of dollars of campaign funds purposely spreading false information, running ads he knew were false, and convincing millions of Americans that the election was corrupt and that he was the true President. As you will see, this misinformation campaign provoked the violence on January 6th."

"In our third hearing, you will see that President Trump corruptly planned to replace the Attorney General of the United States so the US Justice Department would spread his false stolen election claims. In the days before January 6th, President Trump told his top Justice Department officials quote, 'Just say the election was corrupt and leave the rest to me and the Republican Congressmen'. Senior Justice Department officials, men he had appointed, told him they could not do that because it was not true. So President Trump decided to replace them. He offered Jeff Clark, an environmental lawyer at the Justice Department, the job of acting Attorney General. President Trump wanted Mr. Clark to take a number of steps including sending this letter to Georgia and five other states saying the US Department of Justice had quote, 'identified significant concerns that may have impacted the outcome of the election'. This letter is a lie. The Department of Justice had in fact repeatedly told President Trump exactly the opposite, that they had investigated his stolen election allegations and found no credible fraud that could impact the outcome of the election. This letter and others like it would have urged multiple states to withdraw their official and lawful electoral votes for Biden. Acting Deputy Attorney General Richard Donoghue described Jeff Clark's letter this way, quote, 'this would be a grave step for the department to take and could have tremendous constitutional, political, and social ramifications for this country'. The committee agrees with Mr. Donoghue's assessment. Had Clarke assumed the role of Attorney General in the days before January 6th and issued these letters, the ramifications could indeed have been grave. Mr. Donoghue also said this about Clark's plan."

[multimedia]
Richard Donoghue: "And I recall toward the end saying what you're proposing is nothing

less than the United States Justice Department meddling in the outcome of a Presidential election."

Liz Cheney: "In our hearings, you will hear firsthand how the senior leadership of the Department of Justice threatened to resign, how the White House counsel threatened to resign, and how they confronted Donald Trump and Jeff Clark in the Oval Office. The men involved, including Acting Attorney General Jeff Rosen and Acting Deputy Attorney General Richard Donoghue were appointed by President Trump. These men honored their oaths of office. They did their duty. And you will hear from them in our hearings. By contrast, Jeff Clark has invoked his Fifth Amendment privilege against self-incrimination and refused to testify. Representative Scott Perry, who is also involved in trying to get Clark appointed as Attorney General, has refused to testify here. As you will see, Representative Perry contacted the White House in the weeks after January 6th to seek a Presidential pardon. Multiple other Republican Congressmen also sought Presidential pardons for their roles in attempting to overturn the 2020 election. In our fourth hearing, we will focus on President Trump's efforts to pressure Vice President Mike Pence to refuse to count electoral votes on January 6th. Vice President Pence has spoken publicly about this."

[multimedia]
Mike Pence: "President Trump is wrong. I had no right to overturn the election. The presidency belongs to the American people and the American people alone. And frankly, there is no idea more un-American than the notion that any one person could choose the American President."

Liz Cheney: "What President Trump demanded that Mike Pence do wasn't just wrong, it was illegal and it was unconstitutional. You will hear this in great detail from the Vice President's former general counsel. Witnesses in these hearings will explain how the former Vice President and his staff informed President Trump over and over again that what he was pressuring Mike Pence to do was illegal. As you will hear, President Trump engaged in a relentless effort to pressure Pence, both in private and in public. You will see the evidence of that pressure from multiple witnesses live and on video. Vice President Pence demonstrated his loyalty to Donald Trump consistently over four years, but he knew that he had a higher duty to the United States Constitution. This is testimony from the Vice President's chief of staff."

[multimedia]

Marc Short: "That's why I think the Vice President was proud of his four years of service and he felt like much had been accomplished in those four years. And I think he was proud to have stood beside the President for all that has been done. But I think he ultimately knew that his fidelity to the Constitution was his first and foremost oath. And — and that's — that's what he articulated publicly. And I think that that's what he felt."

Unknown: "His fidelity to the Constitution was more important than his fidelity to President Trump and his desires —"

Marc Short: "— The oath he took."

Unknown: "Yes."

Liz Cheney: "You'll also hear about a lawyer named John Eastman. Mr. Eastman was deeply involved in President Trump's plans. You'll hear from former fourth circuit federal judge Michael Luttig, a highly respected leading conservative judge. John Eastman clerked for Judge Luttig.

Judge Luttig provided counsel to the Vice President's team in the days before January 6th. The judge will explain how Eastman quote, 'Was wrong at every turn.' And you will see the email exchanges between Eastman and the Vice President's counsel as the violent attack on Congress was underway. Mr. Jacob said this to miss — Mr. Eastman, 'Thanks to your bullshit, we are under siege.'

"You will also see evidence that John Eastman did not actually believe the legal position he was taking. In fact, a month before the 2020 election, Eastman took exactly the opposite view on the same legal issues. In the course of the Select Committee's work to obtain information from Mr. Eastman, we have had occasion to present evidence to a federal judge. The judge evaluated the facts and he reached the conclusion that President Trump's efforts to pressure Vice President Pence to act illegally by refusing to count electoral votes likely violated two federal criminal statutes. And the judge also said this. If Dr. Eastman and President Trump's plan had worked, it would have permanently ended the peaceful transition of power, undermining American democracy and the Constitution. If the country does not commit to investigating and pursuing accountability for those responsible, the court fears January 6th will repeat itself.

"Every American should read what this federal judge has written. The same judge, Judge Carter, issued another decision on Tuesday night just this week indicating that John Eastman and other Trump lawyers knew that their legal arguments had no real chance of success in court. But they relied on those arguments anyway to try to quote, 'Overturn a democratic election.' And you will hear that while Congress was under attack on January 6th and the hours following the violence, the Trump legal team in the Willard Hotel war room continued to work to halt the count of electoral votes.

"In our fifth hearing, you will see evidence that President Trump corruptly pressured state legislators and election officials to change election results. You will hear additional details about President Trump's call to Georgia officials urging them to quote, 'Find 11,780 votes,' votes that did not exist. And his efforts to get states to rescind certified electoral slates without factual basis and contrary to law. You will hear new details about the Trump campaign and other Trump associates' efforts to instruct Republican officials in multiple states to create intentionally false electoral slates and transmit those slates to Congress, to the Vice President, and the National Archives, falsely certifying that Trump won states he actually lost.

"In our final two June hearings, you will hear how President Trump summoned a violent mob and directed them illegally to march on the United States Capitol. While the violence was underway President Trump failed to take immediate action to stop the violence and instruct his supporters to leave the Capitol. As we present these initial findings, keep two points in mind. First, our investigation is still ongoing. So what we make public here will not be the complete set of information we will ultimately disclose. And second, the Department of Justice is currently working with cooperating witnesses and has disclosed to date only some of the information it has identified from encrypted communications and other sources.

"On December 18th, 2020, a group including General Michael Flynn, Sidney Powell, Rudy Giuliani, and others visited the White House. They stayed late into the evening. We know that the group discussed a number of dramatic steps, including having the military seize voting machines and potentially rerun elections. You will also hear that President Trump met with that group alone for a period of time before White House lawyers and other staff discovered the group was there and rushed to intervene. A little more than an hour after Ms. Powell, Mr. Giuliani, General Flynn, and the others finally left the White House, President Trump sent the tweet on the screen now telling people to come to Washington on January 6th. Be there, he instructed them. Will be wild. As you will see, this was a pivotal moment.

"This tweet initiated a chain of events. The tweet led to the planning for what occurred on January 6th, including by the Proud Boys who ultimately led the invasion of the Capitol and the violence on that day. The indictment of a group of Proud Boys alleges that they planned quote, 'To oppose by force the authority of the government of the United States.' And according to the Department of Justice, on January 6th, 2021, the defendants directed, mobilized, and led members of the crowd onto the Capitol grounds and into the Capitol leading to the dismantling of metal barricades, the destruction of property, the breaching of the Capitol building, and the assaults on law enforcement. Although certain former Trump officials have argued that they did not anticipate violence on January 6th, the evidence suggests otherwise. As you will see in our hearings, the White House was receiving specific reports in the days leading up to January 6th, including during President Trump's ellipse rally indicating that elements in the crowd were preparing for violence at the Capitol. And on the evening of January 5th, the President's close adviser Steve Bannon said this on his podcast."

[multimedia]
<u>Steve Bannon</u>: "All hell is going to break loose tomorrow. Just understand this. All hell is going to break loose tomorrow."

<u>Liz Cheney</u>: "As part of our investigation we will present information about what the White House and other intelligence agencies knew and why the Capitol was not better prepared. But we will not lose sight of the fact that the Capitol Police did not cause the crowd to attack. And we will not blame the violence that day — violence provoked by Donald Trump — on the officers who bravely defended all of us.

"In our final hearing, you will hear a moment by moment account of the hours long attack from more than half a dozen White House staff both live in the hearing room and via videotape testimony. There's no doubt that President Trump was well aware of the violence as it developed. White House staff urged President Trump to intervene and call off the mob. Here is a document written while the attack was underway by a member of the White House staff advising what the President needed to say. Quote, 'Anyone who entered the Capitol without proper authority should leave immediately.' This is exactly what his supporters on Capitol Hill and nationwide were urging the President to do. He would not. You will hear that leaders on Capitol Hill begged the President for help including Republican Leader McCarthy, who was quote, 'Scared', and called multiple members of President Trump's family after he could not persuade the President himself.

"Not only did President Trump refuse to tell the mob to leave the Capitol, he placed no call to any element of the United States government to instruct that the Capitol be defended. He did not call his Secretary of Defense on January 6th. He did not talk to his Attorney General. He did not talk to the Department of Homeland Security. President Trump gave no order to deploy the National Guard that day. And he made no effort to work with the Department of Justice to coordinate and disp — and deploy law enforcement assets. But Vice President Pence did each of those things. For example, here is what General Milley, the Chairman of the Joint Chiefs of Staff testified to this committee."

[multimedia]

Mark Milley: "There were two — two or three calls with Vice President Pence. He was very animated and he issued very explicit, very direct, unambiguous orders. There was no question about that. And — and he was — and — and I can give you the exact quotes I guess from some of our records somewhere. But he was very animated, very direct, very firm. And to Secretary Miller, get the military down here. Get the Guard down here, put down this situation, etc.'"

Liz Cheney: "By contrast here is General Milley's description of his conversation with President Trump's Chief of Staff Mark Meadows on January 6th."

[multimedia]
Mark Milley: "He said we have — we have to kill the narrative that the Vice President is making all the decisions. We need to establish the narrative that, you know, that the President is still in charge and that things are steady or stable or words to that effect. I immediately interpret that as politics, politics, politics. Red flag for me personally, no action. But I remember it distinctly."

Liz Cheney: "And you will hear from witnesses how the day played out inside the White House. How multiple White House staff resigned in disgust and how President Trump would not ask his supporters to leave the Capitol. It was only after multiple hours of violence that President Trump finally released a video instructing the riotous mob to leave. And as he did so, he said to them quote, 'We love you and you're very special.' You will also hear that in the immediate aftermath of January 6th, members of the President's family, White House staff, and others tried to step in to stabilize the situation, quote, 'To land the plane before the Presidential transition on January 20th.' You will hear about members of the Trump cabinet discussing the possibility of invoking the 25th Amendment and replacing the President of the United States. Multiple members of President Trump's own cabinet resigned immediately after January 6th. One member of the Cabinet suggested that the remaining Cabinet officers needed to take a more active role in running the White House and the Administration.

"But most emblematic of those days is this exchange of texts between Sean Hannity and former President Trump's Press Secretary, Kayleigh McEnany. Sean Hannity wrote in part: Key now. No more crazy people. No more stolen election talk. Yes, impeachment and 25th Amendment are real, many people will quit. Ms. McEnany responded in part: Love that. That's the playbook. The White House staff knew that President Trump was willing to entertain and use conspiracy theories to achieve his ends. They knew the President needed to be cut off from all of those who had encouraged him. They knew that President Donald Trump was too dangerous to be left alone, at least until he left office on January 20th. These are important facts for Congress and the American people to understand fully.

"When a President fails to take the steps necessary to preserve our union or worse causes a constitutional crisis, we're at a moment of maximum danger for our republic. Some in the White House took responsible steps to try to prevent January 6th. Others egged the President on. Others who could have acted refused to do so. In this case, the White House counsel was so concerned about potentially lawless activity that he threatened to resign multiple times. That is exceedingly rare and exceedingly serious. It requires immediate attention, especially when the entire team threatens to resign. However, in the Trump White House, it was not exceedingly rare and it was not treated seriously. This is a clip of Jared Kushner addressing multiple threats by White House Counsel Pat Cipollone

and his team of lawyers to resign in the weeks before
January 6th."

[multimedia]
**Liz Cheney: "Jared, are you aware of
instances where Pat Cipollone threatened to
resign?"**

**Jared Kushner: "I — I kind of — like I said,
my interest at that time was on trying to get as
many pardons done. And I know that, you
know, he was always to — him and the team
were always saying, oh, we're going to resign.
We're not going to be here if this happens, if
that happens. So I kind of took it up to just be
whining to be honest with you."**

Liz Cheney: "Whining. There's a reason why people
serving in our government take an oath to the Constitution.
As our founding fathers recognized, democracy is fragile.
People in positions of public trust are duty bound to defend
it to step forward when action is required. In our country,
we don't swear an oath to an individual or a political
party."

Liz Cheney: "We take our oath to defend the United
States Constitution. And that oath must mean something.
Tonight I say this to my Republican colleagues who are
defending the indefensible. There will come a day when
Donald Trump is gone, but your dishonor will remain.
Finally, I ask all of our fellow Americans, as you watch
our hearings over the coming weeks, please remember
what's at stake. Remember the men and women who have
fought and died so that we can live under the rule of law,
not the rule of men. I ask you to think of the scene in our
Capitol rotunda on the night of January 6th.

"There, in a sacred space in our constitutional republic, the
place where our presidents lie in state, watched over by

statues of Washington and Jefferson, Lincoln and Grant, Eisenhower, Ford, and Reagan, against every wall that night encircling the room, there were SWAT teams, men and women in tactical gear with long guns deployed inside our Capitol building. There in the rotunda, these brave men and women rested beneath paintings depicting the earliest scenes of our republic, including one painted in 1824 depicting George Washington resigning his commission, voluntarily relinquishing power, handing control of the Continental Army back to Congress. With this noble act, Washington set the indispensable example of the peaceful transfer of power, what President Reagan called, nothing less than a miracle. The sacred obligation to defend this peaceful transfer of power has been honored by every American president except one. As Americans, we all have a duty to ensure that what happened on January 6th never happens again, to set aside partisan battles, to stand together to perpetuate and preserve our great republic. Thank you, Mr. Chairman."

Bennie Thompson: "As we provide answers to American people about January 6th, it's important that we remember exactly what took place, that this was no tourist visit to the Capitol. Most of the footage we are about to play has never been seen. The Select Committee obtained it as a part of our investigation. This isn't easy to watch. I want to warn everyone that this video includes violence and strong language. Without objection, I include in the record a video presentation of the violence of January 6th."

[multimedia]
Unknown: "Grab your bullet. Grab your bullet. Grab your bullet. Yeah. Just be aware, be advised there's probably about 300 Proud Boys. They're marching eastbound in this 400 block of kind of Independence, actually on the Mall towards the United States Capitol. USA. USA. USA. I am not allowed to say what's going to happen today, because everyone's just

going to have to watch for themselves. But it's going to happen. Something's going to happen, Whose streets? Our streets. Whose streets? Our streets. Whose streets? Our streets. Don't need to hurt you. We are on your side. Don't make us go and against you. Must be a brown shirt. Let me stand aside. Pick a side. These are our streets. 20 bucks a pitcher."

<u>Donald Trump</u>: "I hope Mike is going to do the right thing. I hope so. I hope so. Because if Mike Pence does the right thing, we win the election. All Vice President Pence has to do is send it back to the states to recertify and we become president, and you are the happiest people. Mike Pence is going to have to come through for us. And if he doesn't, that will be a — a sad day for our country, because you'll never, ever take back our country with weakness. You have to show strength and you have to be strong."

<u>Unknown</u>: "USA. USA. USA. USA. Cruiser 50, it does look like we're going to have an ad hoc march stepping off here. There's a crowd surge heading east. We love Trump. We love Trump. We love Trump. We love Trump."

<u>Donald Trump</u>: "Mike Pence, I hope you are going to stand up for the good of our Constitution and for the good of our country. And if you're not, I'm going to be very disappointed in you, I will tell you right now."

<u>Unknown</u>: "USA. USA. USA. USA. USA. Get back, lady. Get back, lady. EA 101 priority, we've been passed first on Peace Circle, breached the line. We need backup. What are you doing? Guys, what are you doing? Madam

Speaker, the vice president and the United States Senate. [Applause]

"Cruiser 50, we're going to give riot warning [Unintelligible]. We're going to give riot warning. We're gonna try and get compliance, but this is now effectively a riot. 1549 hours, declaring it a riot. Cruiser 5 to 50, be advised Capitol Police One advised they're trying to breach and get to the Capitol. 50, I copy. Hold the line. Hold the line. Hold the line. Hold the line. Hold the line. 42, we're about five minutes out. We're trying to make our way through all this. [Unintelligible]

"Go, go, go, go, go. Cruiser 50, we have a breach of the Capitol, breach of the Capitol from the upper level. Be advised, they are requesting additional resources on the east side, as they have broken into that window and they're trying to kick it in."

<u>Jim McGovern</u>: "Without objection, the chair declares the House in recess pursuant to clause 12B of Rule One."

<u>Unknown</u>: "Mike Pence didn't have the courage to do what should have been done to protect our country and our Constitution giving states a chance certify a corrected set of facts, not the fraudulent or inaccurate ones, which they were asked to previously certify. The US demands the truth. Bring out Pence. Bring him out. Bring out Pence. Bring him out. Bring out Pence. Hang Mike Pence. Hang Mike Pence. Hang Mike Pence. Hang Mike Pence. You pepper sprayed another American. We'll fight for you. [Unintelligible]

"Take it all away. Get him back in. Our house. Our house. Our house. Move, move. Our house. Whose house? Our house. Our house. Get the fuckers. [Unintelligible] We can't hold this. We're going to get too many fucking people here. Look at this fucking vantage point. Man, we're fucked. We are area for the housing members. They're all walking over now through the tunnel. We need area 4B. House members, they're all walking over now through the tunnels. Now, now, now.

"We're trying to hold the upper deck. We are trying to hold the upper deck now. We need to close the doors of the Capitol. I need more support. [Unintelligible] We've lost the line. We've lost the line. All MPD get back. All MPD pull back up to the upper deck. All MPD pull back to the upper deck ASAP. Nancy, Nancy, Nancy, Nancy, Nancy. Nancy Pelosi, Speaker of the House. Conductors or [Unintelligible], be advised that capitol police are going to start moving their resources inside. They're going to start at the N4 officers first. [Unintelligible] No violence. No violence. [Unintelligible] Reach 208 with the four members, the door's barricaded. There's people flooding the hallways outside and we have no way out. If I ask officers still remaining on the House floor in the — on the third floor to use the subways themselves.

"It's time to evacuate. Then we can secure the members on the other side. Copy? It's up to us people now, the American people. But what are you ready to do? One more time? What are you ready to do? Whatever it takes. I'll lay my life down if it takes. Absolutely. That's why we showed up today. Bring her out here.

We're coming in if you don't bring her out. Fuck you, you son of a bitch. Bring her out. You back up. Go ahead and try. Get him up. Get him up. Get a medic. Officer down, get him up. Get him up. Get him up. Get him up. USA. USA. USA. USA. [Unintelligible] [Unintelligible] for backup. I need backup. I need backup. Back up. Back up. [Unintelligible]"

Donald Trump: "They were peaceful people. These were great people. The crowd was unbelievable. And I mentioned the word love. The love — the love in the air, I've never seen anything like it."

Bennie Thompson: "Pursuant to the order of the committee of tonight, the chair declares the committee in recess for a period of approximately 10 minutes. [Recess] The committee will be in order. I want to thank our witnesses for being with us this evening to share their firsthand accounts of that terrible day. I know that some of the witnesses from our first hearing are in the room with us along with some of the family members, friends, and widows of the officers who lost their lives as a result of the attack. Thank you all for being here for us and the American people.

"Officer Carolyn Edwards has been with the United States Capitol Police since 2017. On January 6th, Officer Edwards was assigned to the first responder unit which serves as the first line of defense at the Capitol complex. She also served as a member of the Civil Disturbance Unit, a special subset of the uniformed division trained to respond to mass demonstration events. Officer Edwards is a graduate of the University of Georgia and currently is working on a Master's degree in intelligence analysis from Johns Hopkins University.

"Nick Quested is an acclaimed filmmaker who credits include documenting stories from war zones in Afghanistan, Syria, and Iraq. On January 6th Mr. Quested was working on a documentary about quote, 'Why Americans are so divided when Americans have so much in common,' end quote. During that day, Mr. Quested interviewed and documented movements of the people around the Capitol, including the first moments of the violence against the Capitol Police and the chaos that en — ensued. I will now swear in our witnesses. The witnesses will please stand and raise your right hand. Do you swear and affirm on the penalty of perjury that the testimony you're about to give is the truth, the whole truth, and nothing but the truth so help you God? Let the record reflect the witnesses answered in the affirmative. Without objection, the witnesses' statement will be included in the record.

"Pursuant to Section 5c8 of House Resolution 503 I recognize myself for questioning. As you saw just a few minutes ago, the Proud Boys instigated the first breach of the Capitol just before 1:00 PM where rioters pushed over barricades near the peace circle at the foot of the Capitol. Our two witnesses tonight were both there at the time of that first breach. Officer Edwards was standing with other officers behind a line of bike racks that marked the perimeter of the Capitol grounds. She bravely tried to prevent an angry crowd from advancing on the Capitol.

"Unfortunately, she was overrun and knocked unconscious as the crowd advanced on the Capitol. Mr. Quested was a few yards away from Officer Edwards taking footage of the Proud Boys as part of his work on a documentary film. Most of his footage has never been shown publicly before we shared it this evening. Off — Officer Edwards, I'd like to start by asking if you could tell us why you believe it's important for you to share your story this evening with the committee and the American public. Please, your microphone."

Caroline Edwards: "Well thank you, Mr. Chairman. I — I really appreciate it. And thank you to the committee for having me here to testify. I was called a lot of things on January 6th, 2021 and the days thereafter. I was called Nancy Pelosi's dog, called incompetent, called a hero and a villain. I was called a traitor to my country, my oath, and my constitution. In actuality, I was none of those things. I was an American standing face to face with other Americans asking myself how many times — many, many times how we had gotten here. I had been called names before, but never had my patriotism or duty been called into question. I, who got up every day no matter how early the hour or how late I got in the night before, to put on my uniform and to protect America's symbol of democracy."

Caroline Edwards: "I who spent countless hours in the baking sun and freezing snow to make sure that America's elected officials were able to do their job. I whose literal, blood, sweat, and tears were shed that day defending the building that I spent countless holidays and weekends working in. I am the proud granddaughter of a marine that fought in the Battle of the Chosen Reservoir in the Korean War. I think of my papa often in these days, how he was so young and thrown into a battle he never saw coming, and answered the call at a great personal cost.

"How he lived the rest of his days with bullets and shrapnel in his legs, but never once complained about his sacrifice. I would like to think that he would be proud of me. Proud of his granddaughter that stood her ground that day and continued fighting even though she was wounded like he did many years ago. I am my grandfather's granddaughter. Proud to put on a uniform and serve my country. They dared to question my honor. They dared to question my loyalty. And they dared to question my duty. I'm a proud American and I will gladly sacrifice everything to make sure that the America, my grandfather defended is here for many years to come. Thank you."

Bennie Thompson: "Officer Edwards, your story and your service is important. And I thank you for being here tonight. Mr. Quested, I'll also like to ask you to introduce yourself. Can you tell us how you found yourself in Washington DC on January 6th, 2021?"

Nick Quested: "Good evening Chair and Madam Vice Chair. Thank you for the introduction. As stated, in the winter of 2020, I was working on a documentary. As part of that documentary I filmed several rallies in Washington DC on December the 11th and December the 12th and I learned there would be a rally on the Mall and — on January 6th. So my three colleagues and I came down to document the rally. According to the permit, the event there was going to be a rally at the Ellipse.

"We arrived at the Mall and observed a large contingent of Proud Boys marching towards the Capitol. We filmed them and almost immediately I was separated from my colleagues. I documented the crowd turn from protesters to rioters to insurrectionists. I was surprised at the size of the group, the anger, and the profanity. And for anyone who didn't understand how violent that event was, I saw it, I documented it, and I experienced it. I heard incredibly aggressive chanting and I shared — subsequently shared that footage with the authorities. I'm here today pursuant to a House subpoena. Thank you so much."

Bennie Thompson: "Thank you, Mr. Quested. The Select Committee has conducted extensive investigative work to understand what led the proud boys and other rioters to the Capitol on January 6th. We've obtained substantial evidence showing that the President's December 19th tweet, calling his followers to Washington DC on January 6th, energized individuals from the Proud Boys and others extremist groups. I'd like to play a brief video highlighting some of this evidence."

[multimedia]

Marcus Childress: "My name is Marcus Childress and I'm an investigative counsel for the Select Committee to investigate the January 6th attack on the United States Capitol."

Donald Trump: "What do you want to call him? Give me a name. [crosstalk] Stand back and stand by —"

Marcus Childress: "After he made this comment, Enrique Tarrio, then chairman of the Proud Boys, said on Parler, 'Standing by sir'. During our investigation, we learned that this comment during the Presidential debate actually led to an increase in membership in the Proud Boys."

Unknown: "Would you say that Proud Boys numbers increased after the stand back, stand by comment?"

Jeremy Bertino: "Exponentially. I'd say tripled probably."

Unknown: "With the potential for a lot more eventually."

Candyce Phoenix: "And did you ever sell any stand back and stand by merchandise?"

Enrique Tarrio: "Uh, one of the vendors on my page actually beat me to it, but I wish I would have — I wish I would have made a stand back, stand by shirt."

Marcus Childress: "On December 19th, President Trump tweeted about the January

6th rally and told attendees, be there, will be wild. Many of the witnesses that we interviewed were inspired by the President's call and came to DC for January 6th, but the extremists, they took it a step further. They viewed this tweet as a call to arms. A day later the Department of Justice describes how the Proud Boys created a chat called the Ministry of Self-defense Leadership Chat. In this chat, the Proud Boys established a command structure in anticipation of coming back to DC on January 6th. The Department of Justice describes Mr. Tarrio coming into possession of a document called the 1776 Returns, which describes individuals occupying key buildings around the United States Capitol. The Oath Keepers are another group that the committee investigated."

Unknown: "You better get your ass to DC folks this Saturday."

Stewart Rhodes: "If you don't, there's gonna be no more republic. But we're not gonna let that happen. It's not even if. It's either President Trump has encouraged and bolstered strength and to do what he must do or we wind up in a bloody fight. We all know that the fight's coming."

Marcus Childress: "The Oath Keepers began planning to block the peaceful transfer of power shortly after the November 3rd election. And according to the Department of Justice, Stewart Rhodes, the Oath Keeper's leader said to his followers that, 'we were not going to get through this without a civil war'. In response to the December 19th, 2020 tweet by President Trump, the Oath Keepers focused on January

6th in Washington DC. In response to the tweet, one member of the President of the Florida chapter put on social media, the President called us to the Capitol, he wants us to make it wild. The goal was for the Oath Keepers to be called to duty so that they could keep the President in power although President Trump had just lost the election. The committee learned that the Oath Keepers set up quick reaction forces outside of the city and Virginia where they stored arms. The goal of these quick reaction forces was to be on standby just in case President Trump invoked the Insurrection Act."

<u>Unknown</u>: "Did the Oath Keepers ever provide weapons to members?"

<u>Stewart Rhodes</u>: "I'm going to decline to answer that question and grounds — for a due process grounds."

<u>Marcus Childress</u>: "In footage obtained by the committee, we learned that on the night of January 5th, Enrique Tarrio and Stewart Rhodes met in a parking garage in Washington DC."

<u>Enrique Tarrio</u>: "There's mutual respect there. I think we're — we're fighting the same fight and I think that's what's important."

<u>Marcus Childress</u>: "The committee learned that the Oath Keepers went into the Capitol through the east doors and to stark formations. The DOJ alleges that one of the stacks went into the Capitol looking for Speaker Pelosi, although they never found her. As the attack was unfolding, Mr. Tarrio took

credit. In documents obtained by the Department of Justice. Mr. Tarrio said, in an encrypted chat, 'make no mistake' and 'we did this'. Later on that evening, Mr. Tarrio even posted a video which seemed to resemble him in front of the Capitol with a black cape. And the title of the video was premonition. The evidence developed by the Select Committee and the Department of Justice highlights how each group participated on the attack on the Capitol on January 6th."

<u>Unknown</u>: "In fact, the investigation revealed that it was individuals associated with the Proud Boys who instigated the initial breach at the peace circle at 12:53 p.m. [inaudible] Within 10 minutes, rioters had already filled the Lower West Plaza. [inaudible] By 2:00, rioters had reached the doors on the west and the east plazas. And by 2:13 rioters had actually broken through the Senate wing door and got into the Capitol building. [inaudible] A series of breaches followed. At 2:25 pm, rioters breached the East Side doors to the rotunda. [inaudible] And then right after 2:40 pm, rioters breached the east side doors near the Ways and Means Room. [inaudible] Once the rioters infiltrated the Capitol, they moved to the crypt, the rotunda, the hallways leading to the House chambers, and even inside the Senate chambers. [inaudible]"

Bennie Thompson: "Individuals associated with two violent extremist groups have been charged with seditious conspiracy in connection with the January 6th attack. One is the Oath Keepers. They are a group of armed, antigovernment extremists. The other group is the Proud Boys. They promote white supremacist beliefs and have engaged in violence with people they view as their political enemies. Members of both groups have already pleaded guilty to crimes associated with the January 6th attack Mr. Quested, as part of the documentary you've been filming, you gain access to the Proud Boys and their leader, Enrique Tarrio. Your crew filmed them in Washington DC on the evening of January 5th and then on January 6th. On January 5th, the night before the attack, you were with the head of the Proud Boys, Mr. Tarrio, in Washington DC. What happened?"

Nick Quested: "We picked up Mr. Tarrio from jail. He'd been arrested for carrying some magazines — some long — some extra capacity magazines and for the — he took responsibility for the burning of the Black Lives Matter flag that was stolen from the church on December the 12th. We — we were attempting to get an interview with Mr. Tarrio. We had no idea of any of the events that were going to subsequently happen. We drove him to pick up his bags from the property department of the police, which is just south of the Mall. We picked up his bags and went to get some other bags from the Phoenix Hotel. We encountered Mr. Stuart Rhodes from the Oath Keepers. By the time I had gone to park the car, my colleague was saying, who'd got into the car with Mr. Tarrio, that they had moved to a location around the corner, the parking garage of the Hall of Legends, I believe. And so we quickly drove over there.

"We drove down into the parking garage and filmed the scene of Mr. Tarrio and Mr. Rhodes and certain other individuals in that garage. We then continue to follow Mr. Tarrio. There was some discussion about where he was going to go. He ended up going towards a hotel in Baltimore and we conducted an interview with him in the hotel room. And then we returned to DC for that night. And a — and what was interesting that night actually was that was the first indication that DC was much more busy than it had been any other time we've been here because we couldn't get into the hotels we wanted to and we ended up at a hotel that, you know, was not as satisfactory as we would have hoped."

Bennie Thompson: "Thank you. So what you're saying is you filmed the meeting between Mr. Tarrio and Oath Keepers leader, Stewart Rhodes, right?"

Nick Quested: "Indeed."

Bennie Thompson: "You couldn't hear what was said, but according to the Justice Department indictment of Mr. Tarrio a participant referenced the Capitol. Now on the morning of January 6th, you learned the Proud Boys would gather near the rally scheduled to take place near the White House. What time did you meet up with the Proud Boys and what was happening when they met?"

Nick Quested: "We met up with the Proud Boys somewhere around 10:30 am and they were starting to walk down the Mall, a easterly direction towards the Capitol. There was a large contingent, more than I had expected. And I was confused to a certain extent why we were walking away from the President's speech because that's what I felt we were there to cover."

Bennie Thompson: "So at 10:30 am, that's early in the day. That's even before President Trump had started speaking. Am I correct?"

Nick Quested: "Yes, sir."

Bennie Thompson: "So how many Proud Boys would you estimate were marching together to the Capitol?"

Nick Quested: "A couple of hundred. Potentially — yeah, I say a couple of hundred Proud Boys were marching towards the Capitol at that point."

Bennie Thompson: "At the time was the area heavily guarded?"

Nick Quested: "No, that was — we — I remember we walked past the — we walked down the Mall, we walked to the right of the reflecting pool and then north along the road that leads to the Peace Circle. And as we were walking past the Peace Circle, I framed the Proud Boys to the right of my shot with the Capitol behind. And we see one sole police officer at the barriers which subsequently breached. We then walk up and past a tactical unit preparing. And there's — you see that in the film where the man questions their duty and their honor. And you see maybe a dozen Capitol police putting on their riot gear."

Bennie Thompson: "So how would you describe the atmosphere at that — that time?"

Nick Quested: "The atmosphere was — it seemed to be much darker. I — I make efforts to create a familiarity between myself and my subjects to, you know, make them feel comfortable. And the — the atmosphere was much darker on this day than had been in these other — in these other — in these other days. And there was also a contingent of Proud Boys that I hadn't met before from Arizona who appeared to wear these orange hats. And had orange armbands."

Bennie Thompson: "So when the Proud Boys went back down the Hill to the peace circle, did a larger crowd start to gather?"

Nick Quested: "Well, no. First of all, we went round to the back and down the steps and we took some photographs on the east side of the Capitol. And then we went for lunch. We went for tacos."

Bennie Thompson: "So Mr. Quested you're a journalist, so you are careful to stick to things that you have observed. But what you've told us is highly relevant. Let me highlight a few key facts that you and others have provided the committee. First, there was a large group of Proud Boys present at the Capitol. We know that from multiple sources. You now estimate that there were around 250 to 300 individuals that — you've testified. They weren't there for President Trump's speech. We know this because they left that area to march toward the Capitol before the speech began. They walked around the Capitol that morning.

"I'm concerned this allowed them to see what defenses were in place and where weaknesses might be. And they decided to launch their attack at the peace — peace circle, which is a front door of the Capitol complex. It's the first security perimeter that those marching from the ellipse would have to come to as they move toward the Capitol. The peace circle walk away was — walkway was always where the thousands of angry Trump supporters would arrive after President Trump sent them from the ellipse. The Proud Boys timed their attack to the moments before the start of the joint session in the Capitol, which is also where President Trump directed the angry mob. Quote, 'We fight like hell,' end quote. He told them before sending them down Pennsylvania Avenue right to where the Proud Boys gathered and where you were filming.

"Now a central question is whether the attack on the Capitol was coordinated and planned. What you witnessed is what a coordinated and planned effort would look like. It was the culmination of a months' long effort spearheaded by President Trump. Mr. Quested, thank you for your eyewitness account of the lead up to the breach of the peace circle. This brings us to a point in time where you and Officer Edwards were in close proximity. At this point, I reserve the balance of my time pursuant to 5c Section eight of House Resolution 503. The Chair recognizes that gentlewoman from Wyoming, Ms. Cheney, for questioning."

Liz Cheney: "Thank you very much, Mr. Chairman. Officer Edwards I want to start by thanking you for your service and thank you for your courage. Thank you for being here this evening. I know that it's not easy to relive what happened for you and — and for the officers behind you and for the family members of officers in — in the audience this evening. But it's — it's really important for the country to have a full accounting and understand what happened. I want to start Officer Edwards with a short clip that shows the horrible moment when you were injured as the peace circle was breached."

[multimedia]
Unknown: "USA, USA, USA. Move. Move."

Liz Cheney: "Officer Edwards, can you describe the crowd that had assembled at the peace circle as — as you and your fellow officers stood behind and guarded the bike racks at the peace circle?"

Caroline Edwards: "Yes. So there were about — I want to say about five of us on that line. And there were — so there was our bike rack and then at the bottom of the Pennsylvania Avenue walkway right by peace circle there was another bike rack. And so the crowd had kind of gathered there. It was the crowd led by Joseph Biggs. And they were mostly in civilian clothes. There were some who had military fatigues on. We could see people with bulletproof vests on, you know, things like that. They didn't seem, you know, extremely cohesive, but they had gathered there in their outfits. But they had gathered there together.

"And Joseph Biggs started. He had a mic, or a megaphone. And he started talking about, you know, first it was things kind of relating to Congress. And then the tables started turning once the — what is now that the — the Arizona group is what you said — the crowd with orange hats.

They came up chanting F-U-C-K Antifa. And they joined that group. And once they joined that group, Joseph Biggs' rhetoric turned to the Capitol Police. He started asking us questions like you've — you didn't miss a paycheck during the pandemic. Mentioning stuff about our pay scale was mentioned. And, you know, started turning the tables on us.

"And I've worked I can, you know, conservatively say probably hundreds of civil disturbance events. I know when I'm being turned into a villain. And that's when I turned to my Sergeant and I stated the — the understatement of the century. I said, 'Sarge, I think we're going to need a few more people down here.' And so after that, you know, I think they started conferring. They went a little silent. They started conferring among ano — each other. I saw the person now identified as Ryan Samsel. He put his arm around Joseph Biggs and they were talking. And then they started approaching the first barricade. They ripped the first barricade down and they approached our bike racks. You know, at that time We started holding on, grabbing the bike racks. You know, there weren't many of us, so I grabbed the middle between two different bike racks. And, you know, I — I wasn't under any pretense that I could hold it for very long. But I just wanted to, you know, make sure that we could get more people down and get our CDU units time to — to answer the call. So we started grappling over the bike racks. I felt the bike rack come on top of my head and I was pushed backwards and my foot caught the stair behind me and I — my chin hit the handrail. And then I — at that point I had blacked out. But my — the back of my head clipped the concrete stairs behind me."

Liz Cheney: "And you were knocked unconscious. Is that right, Officer Edwards?"

Caroline Edwards: "Yes, ma'am."

Liz Cheney: "But then when you regained consciousness even with the injuries you returned to duty. Is that right?"

Caroline Edwards: "Yes, ma'am. You know, at that time adrenaline kicked in. I ran towards the west front and I tried to hold the line at the Senate steps at the Lower West Terrace. More people kept coming at us. It just seemed like, you know, more and more people started, you know, coming on to the west front. They started overpowering us. And that was right about when MPD's officers showed up. Their bike officers pushed the crowd back and allowed our CDU units as well as theirs to form that line that you see — that very thin line between us and the protesters or the rioters. You know, at that time. I fell behind that line and for a while I started decontaminating people who had gotten sprayed and treating people medically who — who needed it."

Liz Cheney: "And then you were injured again there on the west terrace. Is that right Officer Edwards?"

Caroline Edwards: "Yes, ma'am. So after a while I got back on the line. I got — it was on the House side of the lower west terrace. And I was holding that line for a while. There weren't many of us over there. And Officer Sicknick was behind me for most of the time for about 30 to 45 minutes that I was down there. We were just as the best we could we were just, you know, grappling over bike racks and trying to hold them as quick as possible. All of the sudden I see movement to the left of me. And I turned and it was Officer Sicknick with his head in his hands. And he was ghostly pale, which I — I figured at that point that he had been sprayed. And I was concerned my, you know, cop — cop alarm bells went off. Because if you get sprayed with pepper spray you're going to turn red. He turned just about as pale as this sheet of paper. And so I looked back to see what had hit him, what had happened, and that's when I got sprayed in the eyes as well. I was taken to be decontaminated by another officer, but we didn't get the chance because we were then tear gassed."

Liz Cheney: "And we are going to play just a — a brief clip of that moment that you've just described, Officer Edwards."

[multimedia]
[Inaudible]

Liz Cheney: "Officer Edwards, I just want to thank you for being here. And — and I know again how difficult it is. I know the family of Officer Sicknick as well, who's here tonight. And one of the things one of the Capitol police officers said to me recently was to ask me whether or not as members of Congress all of us understood that on that day, on January 6th, when we were evacuated from the chamber we're led to a safe undisclosed location, whether we knew that — that so many of you had rushed out of the building and into the fight. And I can assure you that we do know that. And that we understand how important your service is. Thank you for your continued work with our committee and the interviews and thank you very much for both of you for being here this evening. Mr. Chairman, I yield back."

Bennie Thompson: "Thank you very much. Ms. Edwards, can you give us one memory of that awful day that stands out most vividly in your mind?"

Caroline Edwards: "I can. That time when I talked about falling behind MPD's line, I remember because I had been kind of shielded away cause I was holding those stairs, so I wasn't able to really see what was going on over here."

Caroline Edwards: "When I fell behind that line and I saw, I can just remember my — my breath catching in my throat, because what I saw was just a — a war scene. It was something like I'd seen out of the movies. I — I couldn't believe my eyes. There were officers on the ground. You know, they were bleeding. They were throwing up.

"They were — you know, they had — I mean, I saw friends with blood all over their faces. I was slipping in people's blood. You know, I — I was catching people as they fell. I — you know, I was — it was carnage. It was chaos. I — I can't — I can't even describe what I saw. Never in my wildest dreams did I think that, as a police officer, as a law enforcement officer, I would find myself in the middle of a battle. You know, I — I'm trained to detain, you know, a couple of subjects and — and handle — you know, handle a crowd, but I — I'm not combat trained. And that day, it was just hours of hand-to-hand combat, hours of dealing with things that were way beyond any — any law enforcement officer has ever trained for. And I just remember — I just remember that moment of stepping behind the line and just seeing the absolute war zone that the west front had become."

Bennie Thompson: "Let me thank you for your service, and obviously your bravery that you have told the world about tonight. It's unfortunate that you had to defend the Capitol from fellow Americans. None of us would ever think that that would have to happen, but it did. So, let me thank our witnesses for joining us tonight and sharing their experiences with America. Throughout my chairmanship of this committee, I've continuously vowed that this committee will ensure a comprehensive account of the heroic acts on January 6th and that we will follow the facts wherever they lead.

"Your testimony is an essential part of that record and helps us do our job. Mr. Quested, thank you for sharing your footage and your account of the day's events with us. The images you recorded and have shared with the committee do a better job than any of our words in reinforcing the violence of January 6th. We hope that the power of your footage help encourage all Americans to consider how citizens with such — so much in common could viciously brawl at the seat of their democratic government. Officer Edwards, thank you for your brave service, as I indicated, on January 6th, and all you did to protect us and, most importantly, our democracy.

"If you and your fellow officers hadn't held the line against those violent insurrectionists, we can only imagine the disaster that would have ensued. Your heroism in the face of danger is admirable, and your will to continue to protect and serve despite your serious injuries should be an inspiration to all of us. We wish you a continued recovery, and look forward to seeing you back in uniform sometime soon.

"The members of the Select Committee may have additional questions for tonight's witnesses, and we ask that you respond expeditiously in writing to those questions. Without objection, members will be permitted ten business days to submit statements for the record, including opening remarks and additional questions for the witnesses. The witness have just told us what they heard the rioters saying while they stormed the Capitol on that day. Now we're going to hear it from the rioters themselves. Without objection, I include in the record a video presentation."

[multimedia]
Unknown: "We were invited by the president of the United States. What really made me want to come was the fact that, you know, I had supported Trump all that time. I did believe, you know, that the election was being stolen. And Trump asked us to come. He personally asked for us to come to DC that day. And I thought, for everything he's done for us, if this is the only thing he's going to ask of me, I'll do it."

Donald Trump: "We're going to walk down to the Capitol."

Unknown: "Do you recall President Trump mentioning going to the Capitol during his speech? Oh, yeah. So, that's one of my disappointments. He said he was going to go, go with us, that he was going to be there. I know why I was there, and that's because he called me there and he laid out what is happening in our government. He laid it out. But I remember Donald Trump telling people to be there, I — I mean, to support. So, you mentioned that the president — that the president asked you. Do you remember a specific message? Basically, yeah — yes, for us to come to DC, that big things are going to happen. What got me interested, he said I have something very important to say on January 6th, or something like that is what got — what got me interested to be there. You know, Trump has only asked me for two things. He asked me for my vote and he asked me to come on January 6th."

Bennie Thompson: "Testimony & Transcripts When the committee reconvenes next week, we're going to examine the lies that convinced those men and others to storm the Capitol to try to stop the transfer of power. We're going to take a close look at the first part of Trump's attack on the rule of law when he hit the fuse that ultimately resulted in the violence of January 6th. Without objection, and with — with that, the committee stands adjourned."

Made in the USA
Columbia, SC
16 March 2023

13899120R00026